The Day I Learned to FLY

The Unfolding of My Life Purpose

ANA CASBIS

Inspired Forever Books
Dallas, Texas

The Day I Learned to Fly

The Unfolding of My Life Purpose

Inspired Forever Books™
"Words with Lasting Impact"
Dallas, Texas
(888) 403-2727
https://inspiredforeverbooks.com

Library of Congress Control Number: 2020924789

Paperback ISBN 13: 978-1-948903-42-4

Printed in the United States of America

Disclaimer: This is a work of fiction loosely based on some true events. Names, characters, businesses, places, events, locales, and any identifying details from incidents have been changed. Any resemblance to actual persons, living or dead, or actual events is purely coincidental.

Table of Contents

CHAPTER 1:
Restless

The room had a clear, clean feel. I'd stopped in the doorway to peek inside. A Mexican man stood in front of a stove, his back to me. He had a short thin figure and short dark-black hair. He turned before I even took a step into the room.

"I've been waiting for you," he said. It felt as if I knew him, yet I didn't recognize him.

"I don't know what's happening; I don't understand anything," said my soul, taking over my body. We sat around a brown wooden table in the center of the room to discuss religion, God, and life.

Something got my attention. I looked up to see the ceiling opening to reveal a clear blue sky, the sunrays beaming through. The once nighttime was now a beautiful bright day. He looked down at me as he began to elevate.

"Come on," he said as he reached down for my hand. This was the first time I felt free—the first time I trusted. Up until then, every time I had attempted to fly, the fear within me had stopped me. I r been able to get very far. I would stay too low or stop ; I would shake and tremble.

Now I was flying.

We flew over the cornfields in Kansas. I felt passion. The wind ran its hands through my hair; it lifted my body. It was spiritually orgasmic. We landed in the middle of a field in front of a big red barn. I felt powerful, felt great. It was then when I realized my powers.

Who was I?

The next morning, I lay in bed, looking up at the ceiling and wondering if I had been dreaming. It had felt so real. I could still feel the wind running through my hair; my fingertips still tingled . . . what had I just experienced? I couldn't understand what this dream meant.

Life had been so hard this far, and the more I dreamed, the more tired I felt. I would wake up feeling as if I had never gone to bed.

I was raising three boys under the age of eight. I had just miscarried a couple of weeks before—the baby had gone into the fallopian tube. That was when the doctor had found a tumor behind my cervix, and I had begun chemo shots three times a week. I was at my lowest. My so-called boyfriend was in full-blown relationships with other women and was gone often. I was stuck at home taking care of my boys with a broken body, broken spirit, broken heart. The reason I was with him to begin with was not because I loved him but because I thought he loved me . . . all I wanted was to be loved . . .

It had not always been like this.

CHAPTER 2: Memories

When I was a child, my family lived in some apartments out in Fresno, California—ghetto, to say the very least. We were immigrants from Mexico. I was only a baby when I was brought to the States. My memories started around the age of four. My mother was such a happy spirit; she was full of life. Her laugh was so loud and unique. I hated it as a kid, though! One day I was looking into the kitchen as she was having a very pleasant conversation with a friend of hers. I could hear her howls all the way in the living room. The first thought that came into my head was *Oh boy, I hope I don't get stuck with that laugh.*

I could remember the feeling of being happy. No cares in the world. My older brother, Hugo, was my best friend. I was a tomboy. I got dirty, and I didn't care—the rougher, the better. My mother shaved my head because that was what they did in Mexico so that when your hair grew back out, it was straight and slick. I was so mortified. I knew I was a girl, but I looked like a boy! Horrible. But nevertheless, I didn't care, because I had my brother—he would protect me, he was so cool, and everyone liked him. He was funny, the class clown. I dressed like a boy and borrowed my brother's clothes for a while until my hair grew back. Fresno had such a cool vibe, and we had so many friends. I liked the fact that you could roam around without worry—we were able to stay out late and didn't have a sense of fear. There was trust among neighbors. Everyone looked out for each other; it was like a family.

My father was a strong man. He had made it. Not only had he come to this country as an immigrant, but he also hadn't known anyone, hadn't spoken the language, and hadn't had money or a place to live. Within four years he had finally created his American dream. He was the epitome of what *strength* really meant. When I thought of my father, I *felt* strength. In 1992, when we'd been in Fresno for four years, he purchased his dream home. A beautiful three-bedroom house with a window that took over a full wall in the living room. It had a big backyard, and we even had fruit trees: strawberries, grapefruits, lemons. I loved it! We made some good memories there. My mother helping me do my projects and schoolwork. She would make glue from plants we had outside— she was very creative. My brother falling and breaking half of a tooth. That gave him his signature look, I would say. That broken tooth looked good on him. All I could say was that those happy times went away so fast. The memories were just not long enough and were always a blur.

One day in 1993, my mother was so excited that my father was going to take her out for her birthday the next day and treat her. She went the extra mile and put a hydrating facial cream mask on that night. My father worked overnight, so she was left alone. We usually all slept with her—and by *all*, I mean all four of us kids. I had a little sister, who was three at the time, and a little bother, who was one, along with my older brother, who was seven at the time. My uncle Tony also lived with us, but he had his own setup out in the garage, which was separate from the house. It was an extra room on the back of the lot. We also had my mother's best friend, Maria, living with us as well. She stayed in the third bedroom, which was in between our room and our parents' room. The restroom was right across from her room. She had two doors to her room—one that led to the hallway, where all our rooms were, and another that led to the kitchen, which had its own door to go out to the backyard and Uncle Tony's room.

Anyway, Mother was happy that Father would be taking her out to enjoy her day when he got home. It was time for bed, and Mother told me to go lock the door and go to bed. Being a kid, I dashed through the living room, into the dining room, into the kitchen, and to the door. I was afraid, but I was brave. I locked the door and made sure to yank the door toward me to verify it had locked; then I dashed back into Mom's room. I jumped onto her bed, and just like that, I was out . . .

I was awakened by a little shove. "Mija, ven conmigo," she said. I was so mad. I had been sleeping so well, and she had to go and wake me up. Nevertheless, she'd asked me to come with her, so I got up and did just that. Honestly, I couldn't say what time it was. I was practically sleepwalking behind her, down the hallway to the restroom. I was mad she'd woken me. As I leaned my body against the cold wall, my mother proceeded to wash off the mask she had put on her face. My eyes were heavy as I looked at her. *Can't keep my eyes open* . . . I shook when I thought I saw the reflection of something running across the mirror as my mother washed her face, but I just disregarded it because I was half-asleep and probably seeing things. I just rested my body against the wall again.

I was growing more irritated, and my mother was taking her sweet time. I was cold and so sleepy and just wanted to get back in bed. That was when a man dressed in black came around the corner. He grabbed my mother from behind, put a knife on her neck, and pulled her into the hallway. I awoke instantly, the adrenaline rushing through my body. I didn't know what to do. He took my mother into her room, and by then, all my siblings were up. The feeling of shock took over my body. *This is not happening; this can't be possible. Am I dreaming?*

"Dejala ir! Matame a mi! Matame a mi!" My soul was taking over me, and I was yelling at him. I didn't care that he had a knife; I was challenging him to leave her alone and kill me. "Kill me!" I continued to yell at him. I could hear everything around me, yet the background noise had been tuned out. I could hear my sister and little brother crying and my older brother yelling and crying.

Suddenly, my mother yelled at me, and I felt her anger—the fire, the heat that went into my body.

"Callate! Callate la boca!"

I came back into my body, and I suddenly felt scared again and didn't know what to do. The stranger pulled her into the living room. I saw her fall to the ground, and he ran off. I was standing in the bedroom doorway, looking at her but unable to say anything, unable to move. She looked straight at me. The only light was from the restroom; everything else was dark.

"Metete al cuarto hija. Ciera la puerta," she said. My body responded. Shut the door. We sat in a circle and soothed my little sister and brother. I didn't know how long we were in the dark; it seemed like hours—yet minutes at the same time. Time was not time. I couldn't feel. I was numb.

I said, "Hugo, we have to do something. We can't let her lay out there. We have to check on her." He agreed. We hid our little brother and sister in the closet. "Stay here. Don't come out until we come back," I said.

We agreed that we would split up. We would go knock on Maria's door—I couldn't believe she hadn't heard anything. Maybe she was not home. We had to do something. It was dark, and we couldn't see much. *Is he still here?* I wondered.

I told Hugo I would go to the farthest door to Maria's room, the one near the backyard. I was always very brave. I didn't know if the man was still there, and I felt like I needed to protect my brother. He would go to the closet door, which was just across from the restroom. Our plan was to bang on both doors until we woke her up. That was our plan, the only plan we had. I told myself to run. *Don't stop until you get there.* I would have to dash across the living room, the dining room, and then the kitchen. *I know I can do it.* We looked at each other, nodded, and slowly opened the living room door. Once we saw the light coming from the restroom, our courage took over, and we ran. I got halfway into the living room, and my fear started to subside. I had a goal: Get help. Get there. I could hear my brother banging on Maria's door before I got to the other door, which made me run faster. Once I got there, I started to bang on her door uncontrollably, repeatedly yelling as loud as I could, "Mi mamá se está muriendo!" We banged on her door for what felt like hours. She didn't come. I was lost. When I finally gave up, I walked back inside, feeling as though I was floating. I felt like I had split. My body was too heavy to carry. I let my human body go as my soul held me up.

As I walked into the living room, I noticed her lying there. I went to her. I called to her, "Mami, estas aqui?" I thought she was sleeping. I caressed her hair; it felt so soft. My fingers ran smoothly all the way through her curly hair. I sat on her back and continued to caress her hair . . . I felt my hand sink into the back of her neck. I sat staring at my handful of blood in a daze. I started humming, and then I started singing . . . until my soul connected with hers. I felt her soul embrace my body as I sat on her in the dark; it was euphoric. It was an out-of-body experience I would never forget. She held my body tight as I sang to her; she rocked my body back and forth. We intertwined into each other's molecules—we became one.

"No me dejes. No me abandones, porque fuerte no soy." I begged her not to leave me. I was only five. There and then I felt emotions I had never felt before—something so unique it was confusing. It was hard to understand how pain was beautiful. The pain became warm and soothing. And just like that, she was gone, and it felt cold and dark again. I was lost.

I couldn't remember much afterward because I was not there—my spirit was traveling. I left my body alone for a while. When her best friend finally came out of the room, she phoned the police. We were also able to get my uncle Tony. When the cops got there, I was covered in blood. My once white socks were now red with blood. The cops took me somewhere to get cleaned up.

When reality finally hit after weeks of feeling dazed, it was like I was living a different life. I was forever changed.

CHAPTER 3:
New Life

About a month after my mother's death, we were back living in Fresno's ghetto. My father was now a single parent with four kids, ages seven, five, three, and one. My mother's best friend, Maria, offered to help my father care for my little sister and brother until he got back on his feet. He would keep me and my older brother. She moved to Texas with the two youngest, and we stayed behind. Everything changed.

I started attending a new school, where I began to be bullied. I would spend my recess time hiding from those girls. They would make up things to get me in trouble, and the teachers would believe them. Well, I didn't think that they believed them—it was more so that they didn't care. I wasn't the prettiest thing. I was Mexican in a school of predominantly white, light-skin girls with light-colored eyes. I didn't say much. I was too shy. Even though I had once been tough, I didn't feel that way anymore. I felt lonely and weak.

Once I went around picking up roaches I found outside and putting them in a box. "Y'all are going to be my friends," I said to them. I gave them food and built them a house. The next day when I checked on them, they were all gone. I was so sad. My heart felt broken. *Nobody likes me,* I thought.

Most tenants at the apartments I'd moved to were very poor, and mainly Hispanics lived there. With time I made a friend in the apartment complex. Monica was the first true angel sent to me. When I met Monica, I was so happy she liked me. I couldn't wait to get home to be with her. My father worked so much he was never home. My older brother and I wandered around alone most of the time.

My mother had passed away in November, and it was now summer. I couldn't wait for summer break to hang out with Monica! Summer couldn't come fast enough, but when it finally did, I was always with her. She was so pretty and charismatic. Everyone liked Monica. I soon started to make more friends. In the area where we lived, there were a lot of small complexes, and all the kids would come over to our complex and hang out during the day. I had a new, cool group of friends. Among those friends, I met some brothers—five of them, ranging from ages eight to three. They would always come outside and play with us. I started to get really close to them and even cared for the little ones like they were my own brothers, often watching over them. Back in the '90s, parents would just allow their kids to be out all day without even checking on them—whether they were working, single parents, getting high, doing drugs, etc. That was the '90s. Once, one of the five brothers, Mickey, who was four at the time, was playing outside when he suddenly got the urge to go home. I told him I would walk him. My father had warned us many times to stay in our complex and to never cross the street. I didn't see any harm in it. My brother had his own little group of friends and was hanging out with the older brothers, playing soccer. I was used to checking with him— after all, he was still my protector and was still trying to be there for me as much as he could. He was not okay with me crossing the street alone. But since I really wanted to walk Mickey home, Hugo decided he would go with me. We knew we shouldn't leave the complex, but . . . "They always come over here—nothing is going to happen," I said. "We won't tell."

We were halfway across the street when I heard, "Oh no, I forgot my ball."

I quickly yelled out, "Wait for me! We are going to get his ball."

My brother and the others crossed the street as Mickey and I ran back. The ball was sitting inside our apartment complex. We didn't think to slow down—we didn't stop, just grabbed the ball and kept going. We were starting to cross the street when I felt a force holding me back. I felt the wind push me back.

It happened so fast. I looked up and saw a blue shoe with a foot sticking out of it. You could see the bone that had broken off, his body in pieces on the other side of the street. The man dragged Mickey along until he was no more. My heart fell to the pit of my stomach. I stood in shock. I couldn't move, I couldn't talk, I couldn't look away. I could remember my father getting home and seeing all the police cars blocking the street. He was terrified, but the relief was evident in his face when he saw us standing there. We later found out from the police that the man who had run Mickey over was a cynical, racist white man who had been sitting in his car, waiting for a kid to cross the street. This man was already wanted because he had done the same thing in the past.

Soon after, my father decided California was not for us and that we needed a change. I sat there one day playing with a doll I'd gotten for Christmas when I heard a knock on the front door. My father was home at the time, so he answered.

"How would you like to see a loved one, family member, a friend who has passed away again?" the person at the door asked.

CHAPTER 4: Change of Scenery

We made the move to Irving, Texas. I loved the long drive. It was soothing; it was tranquil. It was the most time I'd spent with my dad in a long time. I had always been a daddy's girl. I used to cry when he would leave for work. I remembered looking up at him and just being so proud of him. In Texas, the environment was different. I was reunited with my little brother and sister, but I didn't feel an attachment to them. I didn't know who they were anymore. We moved into a neighborhood that was a lot safer than where we had lived before. Father wanted to find those people who had come to our house out in Cali—Jehovah's Witnesses. He asked around, looked in phone books, and searched for them everywhere. He was not finding them. Meanwhile, things moved fast with my dad and my mother's best friend, Maria—they began a romance, and they got married only a couple of months after we moved to Texas. I was too little to understand what was going on. She was nice enough. I honestly just wanted a mother. I had started to feel that the reason people didn't like me was because I didn't have one. I was okay with my dad being with her. One day, while my father worked on his car, he saw some people walking out in the parking lot, and he went up to them and asked what they were up to. Finally, he'd found who he had been looking for. The Jehovah's Witnesses had assembled to begin their preaching.

I started to go to school. I liked Texas. The other students at my school liked me, and they were nice to me. I started to make friends. Boys and girls. I was still a tough cookie, and I was used to playing with boys. It felt good to be liked. I enjoyed the feeling. I was observant, and I noticed the kinds of people who had the most friends. The pretty ones, the rich ones, the funny ones. I knew I wasn't pretty, and I was too shy to be funny. I wasn't the one who could stand in front of class and make people laugh like my class-mate Tito. I was now in second grade. Even though I didn't fit in any of those categories, little white lies didn't hurt. That was when I picked up the art of lying.

It didn't take long for Maria to start being mean to me. Seemed like she was jealous that my father and I had a special bond. I was the spitting image of my mother; therefore my father had that spe-cial spot in his heart for me. I would do everything in my power to please Maria. It started slowly, the emotional abuse. "Estas fea, pinche India."

It went from that to physical abuse. She seemed to let out all her anger on me. She was an angry woman. Still, I tried to do things for her to get her to like me. She didn't like me, because I was ugly—or so I often thought. I would go to school and hide the welts on my arms. My lies developed from small innocent lies for fun to lying because I had to. I often went to school with long sleeves and pants. It got to a point where I was forced to do all the household chores and cook. I was only a kid, and I felt like a slave. She made me feel worthless. I began to wish for death. I started going to bed hoping for one of two things: to wake up to all of this being just a dream or to wake up next to Mom in heaven. It was hard to live always hiding my pain. I didn't know how to do so.

Being a Jehovah's Witness was also not easy. I had friends at school, yet they were not allowed to be my friends, because they were not in the same religion. They were referred to as *not trustworthy*, and I was not allowed to hold relationships with them outside of school. The only friends I could have were those in the same religion.

I grew older, and I just came to accept reality. This was my life; I didn't understand how my life was so sad, but I settled. Maria continued to abuse me, and I was too scared of her to say anything. When I was eleven, we moved to Grand Prairie, Texas. I found a friend at church, Evy, who also felt broken at the time—she felt abandoned, and her mom was so strict that Evy didn't really like her. We clicked, and we formed a bond. She would listen to me, and she had such high spirits despite feeling broken. She was loved, pretty, outgoing, outspoken, and had so many great qualities. I was sometime jealous of her. I wanted her life, even though she said it was so horrible. I felt like it was much better than mine. She was my best friend, and for years I would confide in her with a lot of what was going on in my life—in particular, the abuse. She was the second angel sent for me. If only she knew how many times she saved my life by just talking to me. She helped me cope. I didn't think she ever realized how bad it was.

My father and Maria would always fight once they were married. He really would try to be a good Jehovah's Witness and would try to talk to God for answers. She was so mean and angry she began to verbally and emotionally abuse him too. My father tried and gave her all she wanted, putting us second at times.

Around 2001, one of Maria's sons was visiting from California. He was at least seventeen or eighteen. At that time, I was only fourteen and got along with him. We all did. All her kids were older than us. One night, all of us kids were in the living room, just laughing and telling jokes. Maria came out of her room, walked not even halfway through the living room, turned, and went right back into her room. My father and her spent most of the time in their room when they were not working, unless we had to go to church or go out preaching.

A short while after Maria had returned to her room, I saw my father storming straight toward me. He grabbed me by the hair, pulled me into his room, and started beating me. I didn't know what I had done. Sometimes I would get a whooping from my dad without knowing why. Maria would tell him things, and I wouldn't know why I was getting beat. He would also take out all the anger he had on me. Honestly, I felt my dad's anger being released in me. I knew it wasn't against me; I knew it was because of *her*. I didn't blame my father. I loved him. He didn't know how to handle his emotions. I later heard that she had told my father I had been grinding and feeling all up on her son, but that was not true. I didn't have that mentality. Their relationship was volatile. My father's depression became more and more apparent.

One night when my father was not home, I heard Maria on the phone. Out of curiosity, I went and picked up the phone in the living room. That was when I realized she was cheating on my father. My father had a feeling something was going on. He asked me to spy on her. I told my father everything I would hear her say and do.

By the age of fifteen, I was numb to her abuse. I wouldn't cry anymore, and even though I knew it made her madder when she didn't get a reaction out of me, which would make it worse and last longer, I was done giving her the satisfaction of seeing me cry. I had done everything to try to win her over. I gave up. I wouldn't permit it anymore. I would detach myself from the situation, and I would leave my body to avoid feeling pain. She would eventually get tired and stop.

I was lying in bed one night, my headphones in, listening to my CD player. Suddenly, the CD player started switching and flipping through different channels, as if I was trying to find a signal to a radio station. It was a CD player—how was that possible? I was scared. Being a Jehovah's Witness, I immediately thought it was a demon. I told my father about it. We threw my CD player away, and we prayed. That was the first time that I started to feel another presence in that house. It was not a good one. That energy scared me. I would tell my dad about what I would see and feel, and his wife would get so mad at me, accusing me of being attached and wanting attention, saying I was a liar.

Weeks went by. My father became more aware of his wife's tendencies, and even though my father knew about her infidelity, in the religion we were in, you worked through such things.

After work one day, she and my father arrived home late. Dinner had been made but was now cold. I knew my responsibilities, so as soon as they got home, I served them. I got up to warm their food. I went to place the plates in front of them, and as I walked off, she yelled, *"Que es esto? Esta frio? No sabes lo que haces?"* She was complaining about it being cold. I felt a flame in me, and the anger burst out of me. For the longest time I'd held my tongue—*enough; no more abuse!* I was tired! It came out of me, and I yelled at her. I couldn't remember the words that came out, but it sure did feel great. That was something my father would not tolerate. That was something you didn't do in our household, but he didn't react. He just sat there. She yelled at him, "You're going to let her talk to me like that?"

He continued to eat. That was the last day I saw her. Her side man came to pick her up, and I never saw or heard from her again.

My father found some things she had left behind. She had been doing black magic. There was a letter he found stating that she was willing to give my father's soul for her happiness and wealthiness. All those bad spirits I'd felt were there because they'd been invited. Once she left, the congregation rallied around us and tried to help us cope. What they didn't know was that she'd left my father in the worst predicament financially and emotionally. She'd wasted his money.

CHAPTER 5:
The First Time

We spent the following summer without electricity, and summers in Texas were horrible. I couldn't help it anymore; I said something to one of the members from church. The congregation came together and donated money to pay off the electricity bill. My father had been too prideful to ask.

I grew relationships with some of the older girls in church. I was getting to the age where boys were starting to show interest in me. Crazy how my father did not trust my friends from school but would allow me to go anywhere with these sisters from church. He must have trusted them because their father was very strict and a pastor at the church. My interest in sex spiked—not only was I starting to hear it from school, but the girls from church were having sex with the boys from church and telling me all about it. One of the girls even met a guy online and traveled to New Jersey to meet him. She lied to her pastor dad, saying that it was a work trip, and met up with this man to have sex. I was introduced to alcohol through these same girls. One of them was married and old enough to buy alcohol. But our parents trusted them. Once, my best friend got so drunk we couldn't go home. Instead the other girls from the congregation called her mom and told her she wasn't feeling good and it was best if she stayed the night. She spent the night in the tub throwing up. They got a kick out of her being drunk. It was funny to them. I got my ways from them; I learned how to be clever with my lies. A couple of months after my father's wife left, we moved out of the house in Grand Prairie and back to Irving.

I really matured that summer. I was going into the eleventh grade, and my body was finally getting its form. I had a nice form, naturally glowing tan skin, dark-brown almond-shaped eyes, and glossy, long black hair. I was about five feet two and weighed about 120. My first day of school, I was nervous. Luckily people remembered me from elementary. I also had church friends. The attention I got was unexpected. Attention I'd never felt before. There were guys trying to talk to me left and right.

That was when I met my high school sweetheart, Trone. A football player, African American, five feet nine, running back, fit, popular, womanizer, and the only one on the team who was still a virgin and proud of it. He was in a relationship at the time with a beautiful Hispanic girl, but it was not serious. I would often see him with other girls. I was not attracted to him—in fact, I turned him down several times. He was too loud, cocky, flamboyant, and not my type. I became a challenge to him. The first one to reject him and probably the only. He continued to pursue me; he would come into my classes in attempts to talk to me. He was a senior at the time, and being the star running back, he got his way a lot. I had a friend at the time who was dating his best friend.

On senior skip day, I went over to this friend's house, where most of the seniors had gathered. Although I wasn't a senior, I fit in with them, and I was finally in the "it" group. To give my friend and her man some privacy, I decided to go into her sister's room.

I was lying in her bed, watching TV, when Trone walked in. I was surprised to see him. I couldn't believe I had not gotten through to this guy. Fuck it. I wasn't doing much anyway—I thought, *Why not give him a chance?* So I did. For the first time, he wasn't that loud annoying guy. We laughed and joked for hours, and that was how we started our journey. Our relationship took off fast. I could tell he really liked me; he put in the effort to make me happy. He was a senior and was going off to college soon.

When we'd been dating for about eight months, his parents went out of town, and we were home alone. He'd planned to make the whole day distraction-free. We spent most of our evening watching movies. It was intense—I could feel the sexual tension between us. It was hard to control our desires. He was nervous, and so was I.

It turned night; he grabbed my hand as he led me into his room.

That night, we both lost our virginities. Although I wasn't sure what to expect, I knew I wanted to experience it with him. Our first time, we took it slow and reveled in the pleasure together.

We became addicted to each other. All we did was have sex. Anywhere we could. The park, the car, outside, the movies—even at the hospital once. It was easy keeping this a secret from my father. He was always busy with church or work.

I wasn't sure when it went wrong, but not long after graduating high school, Trone met some new friends who introduced him to drugs. I started hearing rumors that he was cheating on me. The last straw was when my so-called friend Syn called to tell me he'd come over and they'd messed around. They hadn't gone all the way, but they had made out. I was mad at her, but I was angrier with him. I called him over to my apartment one day after school to return everything he had given me. At that point I realized I needed to work on myself and give being a Jehovah's Witness a chance, take it seriously for once. I knew that what I'd been doing wasn't right—being in an intimate relationship with someone who was not in the congregation. I was convinced that my failed relationship was my fault, as I'd known all along I shouldn't have been with him. My mind was made up. I walked to the end of the street, our normal meeting spot, to hide from my dad just in case.

I was standing beside Trone's car when I felt a familiar grasp. My father pulled me by the hair in the middle of the street. In broad daylight, he yanked me all the way home. He'd come out of nowhere. Once we were in the house, he let me have it. He'd been a boxer when he was younger. I could feel every blow in every inch of my body. I was curled up on my bed in the fetal position, with my hands over my head. My sister jumped in, blocking his blows, and he finally stopped. If he only knew what I'd been doing with Trone for the last several months. I packed my bag and ran away that night.

I called Trone to come get me, and I spent some days with him. His mom was aware I would spend the nights and was okay with it, as long as his dad did not find out.

My relationship with my best friend, Evy, was subsiding. We didn't talk much. She was going through her own thing. We had found out that my father and her mother were talking in a romantic way. We did not like that. It was not a bad thing, though—they had both been single for a while, and had they held the same belief system, it would have worked out.

I had recently rekindled a friendship with an elementary friend named Laritza. I was in need of a place to stay, so she talked to her mom, who agreed to let me stay at their house for a couple of months. I vented to a teacher at school one day, and she gave me a lot of advice on how to get my own rights. Which I soon did. I'd been gone for about six months when I decided to go home. People from church had reached out and convinced me. One day I was in the kitchen washing dishes when I felt sick and almost fainted. My dad saw me and decided it was important to take me to the doctor. At that point Trone and I were still seeing each other, but he was still cheating and doing drugs.

CHAPTER 6:
New Beginnings

At the doctor's office, I found out I was pregnant. I was in disbelief as the doctor told me. Yep, right there and then, I felt like my life was over. My life would never be the same. I didn't know who to confide in—this was not only a sin, but it was also an embarrassment.

I had never had a good relationship with my sister. We were different. I felt that even though we'd grown up in the same household, we lived different lives. She was the pretty, sweet, shy, and quiet one. She hadn't been made to do what I'd had to do. My dad's ex-wife had liked her, and I hated my sister for it. Hugo and I had drifted apart—we were no longer close, no longer best friends. He'd dedicated his life to God; this religion was what he wanted. I had sinned too much for him to be able to forgive me.

So I turned to my sister. I handed her my results when we made it home. The doctor had given me an ultimatum. *"Either you tell your father, or I'll tell him."*

My sister was shocked yet happy. She couldn't believe it. "How are you going to tell Dad?" she asked. I was terrified, and I wouldn't do it alone. At church that night I wrote a note. It simply said, "I need to talk after the meeting—it is important." I had my little brother give it to an elder.

The time was going by so fast. The minutes felt like seconds. When the meeting was finally over, I made my way into a separate room where the elder was waiting. My father came in not too long after. It was the hardest thing I had ever done. Years before, I had dedicated my life by getting baptized. This pregnancy was a sin and had major repercussions. I hadn't been baptized because I'd wanted to be reborn. I hadn't even understood most of it. I'd done it because I'd wanted to fit in; I'd wanted acceptance.

My father did not say anything after I told him I was pregnant, and the elder cut the conversation short, stating we would need to meet again soon to talk more in depth. We rode home in silence. For the next nine months, my father barely talked to me. My boyfriend was not around either physically or emotionally, and I felt alone. I would talk to my son all the time. Although I didn't find out the sex of the baby until he was born, I felt early on that he was a boy. I was happy that I would finally have someone to love. I would finally have a purpose, with or without the father.

Anthoni was born on July 20, 2005, at three o'clock in the afternoon. I didn't know what I was going to do or how I was going to do it. I only knew then that he'd changed everything. My father was in love with him. My older brother adored him. My whole family took him in and embraced him. Everyone in church loved him, and even though I'd committed many sins, they did not disfellowship me. I was still able to talk to the people from church. I was not able to attend outings or interact with them outside of church parties or events.

Even though I had felt broken ever since my mother's death, Anthoni put some pieces of my heart back together. I no longer wished to die or felt that everything was against me, but instead I wanted to live. I didn't know how to do it—this feeling was something new to me.

A month after Anthoni was born, Trone came to visit. My father had left to pick up my little brother and sister from school, so we were alone. He wanted to have sex, and I felt uncomfortable because I knew my dad was coming back. Trone forced himself on me and started to kiss me and grind on me—although I didn't want to, he just had a hold on me. I was weak.

My dad walked in and saw us. I was so embarrassed. He turned around and just walked straight into his room. My boyfriend jumped up, scared—he was always intimidated by my father. He couldn't even walk out the door, so he left out my bedroom window.

That day I decided to tell my dad that I was going to make a life with my boyfriend and that I would move out and get my own place. I had been working, and my dad had bought me a car to help me out. I couldn't bear to tell him face to face, so I wrote him a letter. I was only eighteen years old, and I was terrified of my dad but also had major respect for him.

I left my father's house, never to return.

My relationship with Trone did not last. He became violent, found someone else, and impregnated her. He was going back and forth between her and me for a while, and I was allowing it. It was slowly killing me, and I was back to being the depressed person I'd been before. I stopped going to church meetings, and I decided that being a Jehovah's Witness was not for me. I did not have anyone to talk to. My situation was far too embarrassing for me to want to talk about anyway. I was suffering, and I felt useless, not good enough, and ugly. My plan to have a family hadn't worked out.

I got pregnant by Trone two times after that, and I talked to his mother, who told me it was best to have abortions. I did. I didn't know what I was doing. My heart ached over the decision, but my mind told me it was the best thing to do. I didn't even think to get on birth control. One day he was so angry at me that he beat me in front of our child. He sat on top of me and delivered blow after blow. He called his other girl, and on the phone they both laughed at the fact that he was beating me. I could hear her laugh. That was enough. I loved him, but I was tired of him. He left with her that day. I told myself I would not let him back in. My addiction to him was hard to get rid of. My heart ached for weeks with the thoughts of who he was with, what he was doing, the sexual endeavors I imagined he had. It took me a while to get over him. There were countless long sleepless nights, but one day I woke up and didn't care for him anymore. I was over him.

CHAPTER 7:
A Second Chance

At nineteen, I was working at Wingstop. One day, a group of guys walked in. It seemed like they had just gotten done playing basketball. They were all handsome, but one in particular caught my eye. Before they left, one of the guys came up to me and said his homeboy wanted my number. With excitement, I gave it to him.

We talked for hours on the phone that night, and soon we'd been calling and texting for weeks. Yet we still had not met in person. Finally, he asked me out on a date. He was such a nice, genuine guy with a good heart. He had just gone through a tragedy—he had lost his brother to cancer. We just vibed; we clicked.

The day we finally met up, I tried to look my best. I wore a revealing top and some tight jeans. When I first saw him, I didn't recognize him. I realized I'd been confused and that he wasn't whom I'd thought he was from that night his group of friends had shown up at my job. I was bummed. I had spent so much time talking to this guy. I was already there emotionally, so I figured,

Why not just go with it? I wasn't attracted to him, but his personality was alluring, so it didn't matter. Our first date was great. I felt his genuine intentions, and he was okay that I had a baby boy. We dated very briefly. My baby's father was starting to come back into the picture, pursuing me romantically, and although I'd thought I was over him, I really wasn't. I had just coped with his absence.

My new boyfriend, Brandon, had such a great heart, but after a couple of months, I decided to cut things off. Who was I kidding? I needed time to heal from my ex. I tried to work things out with Trone once again, but it didn't take long for me to realize it would just never work. I decided to cut things off with Trone and work on me. I had no self-confidence, especially after being cheated on, and I didn't trust anyone. I was certain I wasn't good enough or pretty enough. I was never comfortable with myself, so I didn't date much—I believed no man would be loyal to me, because I had a child, and I was just someone they could use and move on from.

CHAPTER 8: Endless Love

On September 2, 2007, one year since our last encounter, Trone came over. I had been celibate for a while. He just had a way of convincing me—I folded so quickly that there was no fight. We had sex that day, and he spent the night.

I knew immediately I was pregnant when I missed my period. I was so disappointed in myself. I was barely making ends meet as a single mother, and here I went again with a man who was unstable. He did not provide for his first child, much less the multiple children he'd had with multiple baby mamas. Deadbeat druggy. And now I was pregnant once again. By *him*. I was in disbelief—how could it be? We had not had sex for so long; then we did for the first time in over a year, and I got pregnant? Shame was overwhelming. What would my father say?

I did what I felt I had to do.

One Sunday night, I looked online for home remedies for abortions. I couldn't afford to have a doctor do it. I headed to a store

I'd gone to often as a kid—my dad's ex-wife would take me. That store was the only place I could find a tea that would help me accomplish what I was looking for. The owner was known to be a witch, which I found out later was why we would go to that creepy store. I sensed that she recognized who I was when I entered. I felt her dead stare and blank expression looking at me as I walked toward her. I asked her for what I was looking for. She brought it to me and gave me directions on how to use it. When I got home that night, I immediately took the tea. I felt nothing and soon fell asleep. The pain was what woke me. I ran to the bathroom. It felt like I had peed myself. When I turned the light on, I looked down and noticed a heavy amount of blood running down my legs. I didn't stand long before I hit the ground.

Without me knowing, my baby boy kept me company that night. His warmth was all that was needed to heal me and bring me back to life.

The next day, still in pain, I woke to my son lying next to me. He had made his bed out of towels and had covered me with one. There was blood everywhere, but that did not matter to him.

At the time I was working in a daycare center at a school. I worked up the courage to go to work as if nothing had happened. My days of acting came into play—I was able to play it off.

Weeks went by, and it felt like everything was getting back to normal. I felt okay, and my son and I were taking it a day at a time. About two months went by before I realized I had yet to get my period. I had figured the tea had taken care of the pregnancy. I purchased a pregnancy test; it came back positive. In shock, I quickly looked up more remedies and methods of effective abortion tactics. I landed on one that I knew would be effective, and even though it was very risky—in fact, sometimes deadly—I was out of time. I got a hanger and shaped it according to how the article instructed. I prepared my mind to take the pain I was about to endure. I put myself in a state of mind focused on no pain. My son was over at my father's for the weekend. The shame I would live with was worse than the idea of death. So I got everything ready. I went in the restroom, took my clothes off, lay in the tub, and spread my legs apart, one leg on each side of the tub. "The faster I do this, the faster I can get it over with," I told myself.

I forcefully jammed the hanger up my vagina. The blood poured out. I felt the shooting pain in my intestines. I got paranoid. I was bleeding uncontrollably. No one was there, and I was in too much pain to even move. I instantly regretted my actions. I lost so much blood I ended up passing out. When I woke, I was drenched in blood, and my body pulsated in agony as I cried and attempted to soothe myself.

I called out to God, "Why me?"

As much pain as I was in, I knew what I had to do. I was barely clinging to life. I needed to get up. I managed to pick myself up. I cleaned up and just put it behind me, as if it had never happened.

After self-medicating with a good amount of painkillers, I spent the rest of the weekend in bed. This one for sure had to have worked, no doubt.

Months went by, and my stomach started to show. I began to wear loose clothes. I started avoiding people, which was not hard, because I was already an introvert. For those I couldn't avoid, I lied and said I had a tumor that was growing. I was still plotting to get rid of it. I didn't know how; I just had my mind set that it could still be done. I hated it. I would talk to it and tell it how much I did. People started to worry about me—I was so big, and they believed my lies. The bigger I got, the more depressed I became. I lived those months in a daze. Like a dream. Once again as if my soul was not in my body.

June 2, 2008, I started to get cramps early in the morning. I'd tried to keep the whole pregnancy a secret; I didn't even go to the doctor because of the shame I had. I woke up that morning with pain. I stayed in all day. I didn't think of what those cramps could possibly be, but I knew I was the cause of them. I was still not taking care of myself, even going as far as picking up alcohol on several occasions. I didn't really know how far along I was, and I didn't think to stop and do the math. It was the middle of the night when I couldn't take it anymore. I decided to get in the tub and just take a bath, with hopes it would help. That night my sister was there and was sleeping in the living room. I didn't want to wake her, so I just lay in the tub and tried to control the pain. The cramps were getting unbearable, and somehow my body had that mechanism to avoid pain—it went into a state of avoidance. What I was feeling reminded me of the physical pain I'd endured often as a kid, and my soul detached from my body. I began to feel the urge to push, and soon after, I looked down into the tub—there was a floating baby. I was paranoid. "He's dead?" I kept repeating. Frozen.

I snapped—all those months I'd been in a daze. The sudden rush of awareness hit.

Within seconds of waking up from that daze, I grabbed my son with both hands and raised him above my head.

"God, what have I done? Take my life—take my life, and give my son his life."

Just like that, the energy rushed out of my heart, through my veins, as fast as the speed of light—yet the sensation, every particle of energy being released from my body, made me feel that time was at a standstill. The energy went into my stiff son's body. My body let out a yelp. I began to sob in grief. I then heard him. He let out his first cry.

My sister burst into the restroom, grabbed him out of my hands.

I woke up in the back of an ambulance. I could hear someone saying, "She has another one in there. There is something else inside of her." As we rode to the hospital, I was spinning, inside and out. When I got there, the nurses realized I had ripped my son off the umbilical cord, and the bag had sunk back into my body. The doctor stuck her hand inside of me to pull it out. The pain of delivering a baby was nothing compared to feeling a human arm inside of me. Because of how much blood I had lost, there was no time to waste, and it had to be done.

My secret was out.

The days that followed were woozy. I had lost so much blood, and I was barely hanging on. The doctor came and told me that she did not know how I was still alive. "You are going to die if you don't get a blood transfusion," she said. I made a choice—no blood transfusion. I knew what had happened. This was my sacrifice. God had answered my prayers to save my son, and even though it hurt to leave my children behind, it was a pact I had made with God, and I had to honor it.

I said no and blamed it on religious beliefs. The doctor did not understand. "How can you be selective with your beliefs? You sin by having sex out of wedlock, yet you refuse a blood transfusion? You are okay with leaving two kids behind." Her harsh but true words resonated. But my mind was made up. She gave me a choice: "There is not much we can do here—you can die here or go home and die there."

I decided to die at home. I didn't know how long I had left, but I for sure didn't want to die at the hospital. So home we went. Time went on, and I only got better.

I worried that my new son, Andrew, had been born with defects, that he was not going to be "normal." Surely something was wrong with him. To my surprise, Andrew was a healthy baby boy. It took a while to feel an attachment with Andrew. I struggled to accept him.

Over the course of a year, I came to love Andrew. I realized why he'd come into my life. Anthoni had become isolated. He had been through so much thus far, and I knew he was depressed—he felt my pain. I believed Andrew knew what I'd done to him and how I'd felt about him when I'd been pregnant, and yet he would always embrace me, wipe my tears away—he would never leave my side. He wouldn't do or say much, but his presence was warm and kind. I felt his love, and without him saying it, I felt his forgiveness. I carried guilt for such a long time. How could I have hated such a beautiful soul?

Anthoni came into my life and gave me purpose.

Andrew came into my life to teach me forgiveness.

I'd had so much pain and guilt in my heart for so long. I felt as if my mother's murder was my fault—I knew I'd locked that door, but that was the same door *he* had come in.

It should have been me, not Mickey.

My father's depression was my fault—I was a disappointment.

But Andrew touched me; his soul was understanding. He was love. He was forgiveness.

CHAPTER 9:
Searching for a Connection

I got used to my new life. I coped with the fact that I was now a single mother of two. I knew that I'd rather be a single mom than be with their father. I caught myself wondering about that guy I'd met at Wingstop—Brandon. I would think about him often, and I regretted pushing him away. With guilt weighing on me, I wished I could go back in time. How different would things have been if I had just stayed with him? I'd imagine what it would be like to run into him. I once even drove by his neighborhood, but I couldn't remember exactly where he lived.

One day I ran into an old friend when I stopped at a Braum's near the area where Brandon used to live. This friend happened to still be in contact with Brandon; in fact, they played basketball on the weekends. I gave the friend my number in hopes he would give it to Brandon. I honestly didn't expect to hear from him. I had broken his heart, and now I was coming back into his life with an additional baby.

Yeah, I'm not going to hear from him, I told myself as I drove away from Braum's that day.

The message I hadn't dared to hope for came. "Hey, this is Brandon. How are you?" Took him long enough, but he sure did fill my heart with butterflies.

He doesn't hate me, I thought. We started to talk again, and not too long after, we went out to eat. I took my kids to dinner with him, and he was clearly uncomfortable. Andrew was still a baby. Nevertheless, Brandon gave me another chance, and we began our romance once again. Times were great for a short while. It was amazing how happy he made me. He had younger twin sisters who were in elementary school at the time. He would bring them over to play with my boys. We were a little family, and the twins became like my own little sisters. Brandon was at my place so often it seemed like he lived there. Everything was going great.

His sisters came over one weekend, and we were all out in the pool. While everyone else was swimming, I got up and went into the house. I noticed Brandon's phone going off.

Up to this point I'd known nothing but love, trust, honor, and integrity from this man. There was not one particle in my body that did not trust him.

"Hey, baby, I can't wait to see you again," the text read.

My heart sank. The anger over the betrayal consumed me. I confronted him. He apologized and claimed he would never do it again. I tried to give him a second chance and wanted to believe his promises. A couple of months went by, and our relationship went from bad to worse. Although he never put his hands on me, I was letting his lie consume me, and I was getting very volatile, so we decided it would be best to end things. During this time, I was living with my sister. She was helping me with my boys, as I was still not financially stable. After I ended things with Brandon, I found out I was pregnant.

Even though we had broken up, I decided to reach out to him to let him know. Although he'd broken my heart, I knew that the man had a genuinely good heart and that if I asked for help, he would help. So I called to ask for abortion money. It had been weeks since I'd last spoken to him. He was happy to hear from me, and when I told him about the pregnancy, I didn't get the reaction I'd expected. He was happy! He begged me to keep the baby and give him another chance—he had fucked up and would never do it again. I believed him. At that time, the lease I had with my sister was ending soon.

When Brandon and I got our own apartment soon after, it wasn't long before I found out he was still cheating on me. I felt like I was dependent on him because I'd had to quit my job to care for the baby. You see, I was an immigrant with no papers, so it was hard for me to find a job. I felt stuck. It was horrible—he cheated so much that I just came to expect it. I didn't understand him; every time he got caught, he seemed genuinely hurt and apologetic. I spoke to many of his side women, who knew he had a woman at home—they didn't care.

I was eight months pregnant at a doctor's appointment, and the doctor asked permission to speak in front of Brandon. I didn't think twice and just said, "Yes, of course."

"Ana, you have chlamydia. This is a sexually transmitted disease."

Brandon's guilt-ridden face couldn't have said more. I couldn't believe it. On top of cheating, he was being unsafe.

I immediately called my sister and told her. Brandon apologized to me the whole way home. It was the same sob story I always heard. Once we got to our apartment, he didn't stay long after our argument. My sister, who was in the area at the time, rushed to my place. But I didn't want to talk or see anyone. She called and called. I rejected her calls. She knocked and knocked. I didn't open the door. Hours went by, and she continued calling and would occasionally knock.

"I am not going anywhere," she yelled through the door, and she planted herself on my front step until I finally opened the door.

"All I want is to be loved," I said.

She simply held me. "I'm sorry this is happening to you. I am here for you." She was my angel during those hard times.

"What did I do to deserve this?" I didn't know what to think anymore. I honestly just wanted something to believe in. I didn't understand life. "Why does God hate me so much? Why do I keep receiving the short end of the stick?"

On December 8, 2010, my son Brandon joined us. Brandon Jr. lit up the whole room as soon as he came out. His energy was a positive one. He was such a beautiful baby. He was in such a rush I almost had him in the hallway and ended up having him in the prep room at the hospital. He gave a nurse the experience of a lifetime delivering her first baby. She later came in and thanked me for such a wonderful experience. Brandon Jr. was such a joy. His father was a proud man. He had his boy. But even then, he did not change. The more time I was occupied, the freer he was. I had many sleepless nights. My little Bee got older as months went by—he was the most positive one of all of us.

I was not familiar with his energy. He would grab my chin, look me dead in my eyes, and say, "Mom, you are amazing! You are great." I always thought it was so cute and wondered where he'd picked up that attribute at such a young age. I started to see my worth, and I started to value myself. I didn't realize what an impact he was making and the changes that were to come.

I stayed with his dad for three more years. Our relationship had progressively gone from bad to worse and could not possibly have gotten any worse than where we were. There was no trust between us, and there was constant fighting. He was an amazing dad but a horrible partner. He was putting so much bad energy into the world with drugs, women, and addictions that it was affecting all of us. Around this the time I began to have weird dreams. I found out soon after that I had miscarried, and I had a tumor behind my cervix. I had to take chemo shots three times a week for three months. I knew for a fact he was with other women while I was stuck at home, in pain and caring for our children. Years later he admitted to me what he had done. However, this time it was different. The energy that my lil Bee exerted was too great, and it did not let me fall into that deep depression, not this time. Instead I started searching the web for answers. I looked for information about God, life, the universe, real-life angels, chakras, the pineal gland, and the law of attraction. My soul was taking everything in. For months I did a lot of investigating and researching. I was consumed by the feeling of not being from this planet. I was just trying to find myself. I started to view myself differently. The three boys' forces were too grand, and they had finally awoken me. More time went by, and my relationship with my now husband was still cold, and our arguments were daily. We'd decided that getting married would help our financial status, as I would be able to work. We had been together for five years at this point.

I didn't want to be with him anymore, so my plan was to get my papers and dip.

It had been a while since I'd last felt real affection and genuine interest. I turned to the internet and used several different apps I had once caught my husband using to cheat on me. Now I was using the same ones.

Fall time was beautiful in Texas, but the next fall that came around was a lonely one. During that time, I met a lot of people, but two in particular would not only change my life but continue to be a part of it for many years.

I met Jay first. When we started talking, it was not sexual like all the other chats. It was spiritual. We both talked about how we felt and what we believed. Our bond was very special—a spiritual connection. He was honest with me from the very beginning and told me he had just gotten out of jail and that he was under house arrest. He asked me to come over one night when my husband was at "work," so I did.

Jay started off by introducing me to his parents, who were visiting at the time. Many years later, he told me that he never did that—introduce women to his parents. I was different. Our connection was instant. We sat in the living room and talked for hours about different myths and conspiracies. We made our way to his room, and it was obvious there was chemistry. As soon as I walked in, the sexual desire possessed my body. The room was dark, so he turned on the light next to his bed. It was a high bed, a queen, the first memory foam bed I had touched. He was so attractive. His skin was chocolate brown, he had several tattoos, and he was five feet nine with a muscular figure. He had a nice gold grill. His presence was that of a boss. It was unbearably sexy, and he smelled *so* good.

That was the first time I tried coke.

He asked, "Do you want a hit?" I had never done it before, but I wasn't worried—I wanted to try it. I had heard of it before, and from what I'd heard, I figured it was awesome. I didn't know anyone who sold it, and I wasn't ever around anyone who just happened to have some. I had only heard stories.

I took my first hit.

A sensation rushed to my head as adrenaline surged through my veins. I felt the wetness between my legs before he'd even touched me. The eagerness to feel him made my body yearn for him.

Our souls remembered meeting before—the memory stimulated our bodies, and we synchronized. His sensuality and desire begged for me. We fucked the rest of the night. As a matter of fact, I came back for more three days in a row. On day three, he had something to tell me.

"Cutie, I hope you know this isn't a forever thing. I'm a pimp, and a relationship is not what I'm looking for." He told me that right after sex. I was confused—not because of what he'd just said but because up until that moment, I had not thought about a future with him. I had just been enjoying him. I didn't care what he did; that was his business, not mine. I had never connected with anyone like him. I enjoyed him, and that was all that I cared about.

I didn't agree with what he did for work, but I did admire his honesty and his broad mind.

He went on to tell me about how his business worked and why he did it. The women who worked for him did so because they wanted to; he did not force anyone. I noticed how women would just hunt him down and do anything for "Daddy."

Jay and I kept in touch, but those three days were all that we spent together at that time.

CHAPTER 10:
A Time
of Waiting

During the day, I was a regular mom doing regular mom things. But at night, I sex-chatted with people online. It didn't go further than that. I liked the attention I got from men. On a weekend night when the boys were not at home, I was online chatting with this guy who happened to be in prison. He went by Kountry. We started a regular conversation. From his picture, I could tell he was very attractive—six feet three with chest, arm, and stomach tattoos. He was an African American with light skin, beautiful light-brown eyes, and a short fade haircut. I liked the tattoo he had next to his eye—a teardrop. I could tell he was a womanizer right away; everything he said was perfect. I liked the conversations we had. I became comfortable with him. I could tell him anything. We talked about life, relationships, men, women, sex, religions, God, myths, and theories. He never judged me. He understood. We talked about absolutely anything—there was no limit, and I felt I could trust him. He told me why he was in prison. He'd been pulled over with paraphernalia on him, which had landed him in prison for five years. Very early on in our friendship/relationship, he would tell me I was an angel. He said he just knew it; he could feel it.

My husband and I moved in with his grandmother due to financial hardships that following summer in 2012. I was a weed addict by then. I would smoke as an outlet. My marijuana addiction caused me to rekindle my friendship with an old elementary school friend, Carlos, through Facebook. He reached out to me and happened to live only a street away. He and I became friends again, and I would often go to his house to smoke. I was not physically attracted to him, but I did like his persona. He stood tall, although he was not much taller than me. He was moving a lot of weight, and something about that lifestyle attracted me. I would go do pickups and drop-offs with him. The environment was appealing to me. The cars, houses, properties, attention, money, and especially the *power.*

Around that time, I worked at a lingerie store at the local mall. I moved up fast and got to a manager position. I grew closer with a lot of my coworkers, and I realized everyone smoked weed. Carlos would come through at least three times a week and sell out. I mean, it was the whole mall—people from every store were his clients. I noticed how much he made—and how quickly. I was observant.

One day Brandon went to work and forgot his phone. It started to ring, so I answered it. No response. I looked through the contents of the phone to find out that Brandon had a mistress who was also married, and they were planning to run away together. He'd met her at work and had developed this long-term relationship that even people at their job knew about. I was hurt—not because of the cheating but because I had been around this girl and her husband several times before. I felt the betrayal from everyone around me who knew about this and had decided not to say anything.

I knew our marriage was over. I told him about the relationship/friendship I had developed online with Kountry, and we decided to split. I moved out, and he stayed behind. To start over.

Over the next year, I slowly reached a better place. I found a good job after obtaining my papers, I had my own place, and my boys were happy. When the boys and I had first moved out after the split, we didn't have anything other than our clothes. With time, savings, and motivation, we started to build a new life.

I was still in contact with Kountry, and it had progressed to phone conversations. We were getting serious. He was a general, meaning he was high up in the gang rakings, so he was able to get a cell phone. While I knew it wasn't good, I liked the power he held. In prison he had so many people under his belt. He was doing time and vacationing simultaneously. He had an organized drug ring, with people bringing drugs in from the outside. He never involved me or asked me to bring anything. He didn't need me when he could get the police to do it for him.

He was in another state, and I decided to pay him a visit a little over a year after we met.

I had a new friend, Ms. Strick, whom I had met through my sister. She was fun, and we went out a lot. I would tell her about Kountry. I didn't tell her where he was or what he did. It was embarrassing to be in a relationship with someone in prison. I introduced him as an entrepreneur who traveled a lot, so we didn't get to see each other often. At this time I was working at a call center and getting along with the people there.

The call center put me through very rigorous training all while studying my personality. Their aim was to identify what worked for a corporation and how to maximize the potential for the best customer service by hiring people who fit the call-center type—to not only work well but to work effectively under pressure. This was a job that could mentally break a person who was not trained appropriately.

During this training, I read a book with some very valuable information about human characteristics. It intrigued me, piqued my interest.

It broke down personalities into four categories:

1) Amiable: They ask for permission. They are timid. They need approval.

2) Expressive: They are loud. They converse using third-party stories.

3) Drivers: They are successful. They get things done. They know what they want and will tell you.

4) Analytics: They analyze everything. They want explanations in detail, step by step. They keep track of everything and are normally good with money.

The information I learned from that book was tremendous, and it helped me in the next chapter of life. Working in the call center, I met J. He was trans. I didn't know what that was at first until he explained it to me. You'd never have known by looking at him. J was uncomfortable with himself; his journey was just beginning. He was a very spiritual person, and his mom was amazing—she supported him 100 percent. J was pure. I felt like I could always be honest with him. He was one of the few people I was able to tell about my powers—my intuition and glimpses into the future—even before I knew I had them.

At this point Brandon and I had been separated for over a year, and our relationship as coparents was getting better. He came over one day in hopes of rekindling our marriage and divulged everything he had done while he'd been with me. He wanted closure. He needed to get it off his chest. He owed me that much, or so he said. I couldn't believe a lot of the things he told me, and even though I was over him, it still hurt to think of the extent of his drug addiction, infidelity, and lies.

Now that Kountry and I were getting more serious, he started to send me money. He asked me to go collect Green Dot cards loaded with money from people who owed him and were paying off debts. At first it was a couple hundred dollars, and soon it became a few thousand. These cards had limits, and each one required a valid social security number. I confided in my friend Ms. Strick, and she knew how to play the system. She knew the right people. I knew she would help me get social security numbers. Before I knew it, I had a lot more cards, and I couldn't keep track, so I kept a journal. Kountry hid his complex and methodical mind. His brain was amazing; I'd never seen anything like it. You see, Kountry had been born into a family of Crips, gangsters. The whole family were gangsters. His great-uncle had created the gang. Kountry was respected, and everyone worshipped him, and he was known to be generous. He was also feared by some.

The first life tragedy that changed him had happened when he'd still been in elementary school. His family went to the town fair. He was one of seven brothers—the middle child. He always felt like the oddball because his brothers would pair up and gang up on him. That day at the fair, he wandered off alone. A generous man found him. The man bought him all sorts of things; he gave him everything he wanted. Kountry's family was poor and never had much, so this generosity made him so happy. The man offered to take him on a roller-coaster ride. On the ride, the man took advantage of Kountry sexually, and there was nothing Kountry could do as he sat there helplessly. He felt disgusting when it was all over.

His mother later found him and whooped him for wandering off. The shame and embarrassment kept him from saying anything to his family. That experience had changed him. He had once wanted to be someone, and now he felt wicked. He'd picked up drugs at a young age and had gone on to commit murders. He told me stories I don't dare write. Kountry did a total of fifteen years. The first time he went to prison was due to aggravated robbery at only eighteen. At twenty-eight, he was released. People didn't know how smart Kountry was—they took him as a thug. He had a photographic memory, I later found out.

Prison changed him the second time around. He found himself. Kountry was a realist. He knew that temptation was a mother-fucker. He knew I would be unfaithful while he was in prison. During my three-year whirlwind relationship with Kountry, I had sex with Jay, whom I kept in contact with for the occasional fuck. He was by far my best. The relationship between Jay and me was just spiritual and sexual. I ended up fucking Carlos one night, and to my surprise, he was not bad. I also talked to an old high school friend who was in college at the time playing football—he was younger than me, so I kept him a secret. Kountry understood and was okay with it.

The first time I saw Kountry in person, I drove out of state to visit him. I asked my friend Ms. Strick to go with me, but she still had no idea he was in prison. I could have gone alone, but I was having car problems.

I wore a skirt that accentuated my butt, a tight shirt, and some high heels. I had mastered the sexy heel walk. I was used to it from my youth, when I had been required to dress up for church. I had some killer calf muscles.

I was sitting in the prison's visiting room waiting for him. I was so nervous. The door opened. I caught a sniff of his cologne. A strong, tall man with the most-beautiful eyes entered. He embraced me and hovered over me. His tight hug and his scent captivated me; I felt as if I'd been in his arms before. It felt perfect. He was strong and big yet soft and gentle with me. I could tell he ruled the pod just by the way people addressed him, from the prisoners to the guards. I could tell he felt superior. We walked around as he showed me off, proud to have me. We spent about five hours together, and the day was amazing.

On the way back from the prison, I was so happy. I got pulled over for speeding, and I didn't have a license at that time, so I ended up in jail. I was still high off the excitement of my day, and I called my friend back at the hotel and told her. She didn't believe me at first—she thought I was joking, but she soon realized I was not. When I got to the jail, the guy who was booking me liked me, so he let me chill in the office with him. Now, this was in a little city in Oklahoma, so it was not like a maximum-security jail. They had a crime rate of around zero. The jail was so small it looked like it belonged in an old, small town. The cuffs would just come straight off my hands because my wrists were so small, so I took them off.

"Ana, you're not supposed to do that." The guard laughed and turned around. He let me use the phone as much as I wanted, and I was able to call Kountry and tell him what was going on. He told me he would take care of it, but before he could, my sister had already been notified and was on the phone with the jail. She had posted bail, and my little brother was on his way from Texas to pick me up. That was a very hectic day.

Kountry's discharge date changed three times. It was another year before I could see him again. He caught an additional charge when they raided his cell and found his phone. I was getting tired of waiting for him, and I couldn't go see him often since I had three kids I needed to take care of. But we continued to stay in touch, even though at the time it felt like we were losing each other.

CHAPTER 11:
Stuck in a Cycle

I really liked the idea behind the law of attraction. It made sense to me, and I gravitated to it. We know what we want, and we manifest it. Kountry also agreed with the law of attraction. My life was where I wanted it to be. My nonphysical relationship with Brandon was great. I did not stay in contact with my high school sweetheart. The man had added two more baby mamas to his life. All three of my boys recognized Brandon as their father. He had maintained a relationship with the boys, and they called him Dad.

I had money saved up in my personal savings as well as the money Kountry had sent. I was ready to start our new life. We wanted to buy a house when he got out. My family knew about him, but they were under the impression he owned a trucking company.

The day finally came when I was able to go get Kountry. I had his clothes, jewelry, shoes—everything was ready for him. I had gone out and gotten him a whole new wardrobe, one that fit him well. When he walked out of the prison a free man, I was starstruck. That man was so fucking gorgeous he made me nervous. He was so affectionate toward me, and I felt sexy. He would always compliment me. While Kountry had been in prison, he'd gotten three tats to commemorate me. He'd gotten his forearm done with an angel—it had my initial and a quote saying, "Multiply my love by infinity. Take it to the depths of forever, and you'll still only have a glimpse of how much I truly love you."

On his ring finger he had my first name, and across his chest he had our anniversary date: 4/17/2016.

I still found that teardrop on the left side of his face so attractive. He was mine. He was known as a player, and up to now, he had never been in a serious relationship, so a lot of people were surprised that he would settle down. The fact that I had one of the biggest bosses in the industry boosted my confidence. I loved the way it felt to be on his arm.

It didn't take long after he got out for me to realize this man was flamboyant, and I did not like that. He liked attention, and he knew a lot of people. He'd run into someone he knew everywhere we went: At one of his family parties. In a houseful of gangstas, telling raw stories. It was there I noticed the respect he got. I started to see his power. I remember noticing and identifying the type of a person he was; I realized this man was a chameleon. He could modify to fit all four personality categories, and he had perfected them. He was a smooth motherfucker. He got what he wanted. I could see the women lusting over him and the men wanting to be him. His cousin told me that Kountry used to carry a necklace made out of the teeth of people he had knocked out—it was his trophy.

It was great having Kountry home. Despite him always being the center of attention when we were out, he wasn't self-absorbed when we were alone. He showed me undivided attention and love. He would wake up early to make my coffee. He would run my bath, give me gifts. He was a real romantic. He did everything to prove to me how much he loved me. After getting out, he decided lying low was best. I was perfectly fine with it. We did not need money.

He was new to me and my kids, but he was great. He loved the outdoors, so we used to go running, biking, camping—we did it all. He was a country boy at heart. Kountry made friends easily. People were drawn to his personality. A few weeks prior to his release, I had been woken up by the sounds of a woman screaming and a man beating her. I'd seen them outside, and I had gotten into a verbal altercation with the man. Unknowingly, Kountry later became friends with the man, who was also a druggy.

Some of our other neighbors at the time looked to be college kids training to be nurses. Kountry told me that they had stolen prescription drugs from the hospital and sold them. I was surprised to hear that, because they didn't seem like that type. I started to notice little changes in Kountry. He started to become jealous. He would often check my phone and even went to the extent to smell my panties to make sure I was not cheating. To a previous addict, temptation was the worst weakness, and his new friends weren't helping.

He started doing coke, ice, pills, weed, alcohol—you name it; he did it. It was just a complete change. He began to cheat on me and started to physically abuse me. Several times I cried to my work friends. I was in the same cycle again of taking him back after he apologized. I was so angry with myself, and I allowed myself to go downhill from there. When we were fighting, I would get urges to push him to his breaking point because I knew what made him mad, and I wanted to hurt his feelings just like he had hurt me. Kountry had patience, but I had anger, and he could take only so much before he got aggressive. He would say I was a giant in a little person's body. Within a year we had lost a lot of money. He was so strung out on drugs.

I got home from work one day, and we started a heated argument. He locked himself in my apartment with all my stuff there and went on a drug binge. I lost my apartment because of it. That night I walked from my apartment to Brandon's house, which was in another city. It took me the whole night to get there. My feet were blistered when I made it. Once I got to his house, I told him everything. I knew that Brandon loved me. He let me move in for a couple of months. I attempted to get my things from my apartment by calling the cops, and they told me they couldn't do anything since Kountry didn't want to let me in, and he lived there. I had to wait until Kountry finally decided to let me back in. Kountry had taken the time in prison to read every law book there was, so when the cops showed up, he knew they couldn't make him let me in. Days after he got off this binge, he called and apologized for what he had done and swore he would never do it again. He blamed the drugs.

What Kountry did not know was that time had provided me with experience, knowledge, and strength. I had saved money and had a bank account he did not know about. I had thousands of dollars in just that one account.

Boss move, bitch. Checkmate.

CHAPTER 12: Entrepreneurship

I decided to quit my job and start a new life. I would open a business with what I had saved.

The business I was about to get into was not quite the one I should have been in. Life had introduced me to certain people, and even though I felt ugly, I was not. I attracted handsome, powerful men. I'd always been good at math, and I'd learned the weed business from Kountry. At the call center I'd learned how to negotiate, and I was good. I was an introvert, which was good because it helped me keep a low profile. I began to negotiate with my connections and sought to find the lowest drug prices in the market by pounds. I then sold it at a higher price in smaller quantities, and I would profit. I started off by reaching out to Carlos, who was low key but moved big. I reached out to another former acquaintance who had moved from city to city. Then I talked to an old high school friend who had a lot of friends, so it was easy for him to sell out fast.

Before I knew it, I was negotiating pricing between big bosses. They would call me to find them the cheapest prices. I was getting calls from distributors, famous people, basketball players, football players, lawyers, doctors, and rich people who lived in mansions. They always needed a shitload of drugs for their parties. I would sometimes deliver it but not always.

Coincidentally, I met a guy from Colorado and another from California who grew their own weed. I was seductive, so I had men I didn't care for wanting me; therefore they would give me what I wanted. I had a manipulative hold on them. I got a kick out of getting men erect and just walking out on them. Men like this were not used to that, so they liked it. They were used to getting what they wanted, so when they didn't, it intrigued them. I loved the attention I got from them. Power felt better. I didn't see any danger in it, since no one was getting hurt.

My older sons moved in with my sister, and my youngest went with his dad. I maintained good communication, but my business was taking me away from them. I used the bad experience with Kountry to my benefit and asked my sister to allow them to stay with her for the summer while I focused on rebuilding myself.

I ended up renting an office that cost me $400 a week. I hired four guys to help me run it. They were like bodyguards. A Nigerian friend I'd met through Kountry was all about money and business. He was a big man, scary looking—someone you didn't mess with. He went by Kongo. He came with three men who were loyal to him. If you took care of them, they took care of you. I didn't have to worry about much. For the next months I lived out of some of the best and most-expensive hotels.

I was in a hotel chilling in the pool alone one day when I saw this guy walking by. He gave me skateboarder vibes. He was a cute skinny white boy. I ignored him as I lay out in the sun. He eventually made his way over to me, and we started to talk. His name was Tony. He had grown up as a Jehovah's Witness as well and not too long ago had been disfellowshipped. The crazy thing about Tony was not only his past as a Jehovah's Witness but also that he was a drug dealer who would move coke from Mexico into the States. The only reason he'd stayed a Jehovah's Witness was to keep a relationship with his mother, who was his heart and was also a Jehovah's Witness. I understood. Tony and I became cool, and we hung out for many days in a row. We would meet in random areas of the hotel. It was fun. We didn't have anything sexual. We would just talk and do coke. His stories about drug deals and the Mexican mafia were many. I loved to listen. After a couple of days, he conveyed that he liked me, but I was not interested and told him I only wanted to be friends.

My last day in that hotel, we were sitting on the floor in the middle of his penthouse snorting white and cracking jokes. This room was at least one hundred floors high. He received a phone call and got up to answer it. He quickly hung up and calmly said to me, "Ana, love, I'm sorry, but my time is up. I have to run. Will keep in touch." He asked for my phone to put his number in. He then leaned in, and we locked lips. It was amazing. He held my head in a passionate way, looked at me, smiled, and walked out the front door. I stood there for a minute. I hadn't made out with anyone in a long time. It felt good.

I waited for the elevator to go to my room. I heard a lot of commotion. The elevator doors opened, and FBI agents hurried past me, not even paying attention to me as I just rushed out of there. I was scared. I was also surprised they hadn't seen me. Tony was long gone, and before they could find me, I had already checked out. I never kept the reservations under my name, so they wouldn't know who I was.

Kountry was in town. He called and asked me to meet him. I had kept very little contact with him. I knew he had stopped doing drugs and was back on track with his life, but I couldn't forgive him. I missed him, but I now valued myself.

I decided, *Why not see him?* It had been some time since I'd last seen him. He took me to an upscale restaurant. We had our own area secluded from the rest. He gave me a white angel necklace with wings made of diamonds. I loved it. I could see the love he had for me in his eyes. The tears rolled down his cheeks as he held my chin up toward him and said those sweet words, "Te amo, hermosa." He'd picked up some Spanish.

"Te amo, mi rey," I replied. After that day, we didn't speak to each other for quite some time.

I had mastered the law of attraction. Or so I thought—you see, what I forgot was that we were not alone. Even though I was manifesting what I wanted, I was not alone, and others were manifesting what they wanted in the same world.

The months went by, and the money was coming in fast. I had started another legitimate business that was now consuming most of my time. I had a creative eye, so I was organizing weddings, business events, parties, quinceañeras—you name it; I did it. I was able to use the same clientele with this business. I did my clients' kids' birthday parties. I carried on conversations with these men's wives—the very same powerful, successful men who had been begging me to get in bed with them. The very ones I might have been in bed with the night before. Powerful men were my weakness. I stayed away from the thought of love. The power I had was greater; love didn't seem realistic.

I was leaving a business meeting one day and decided to stop at a local coffee shop to grab tea. It had been at least four months since I had last seen Kountry. There he was at the counter, ordering a coffee. Black, no sugar. Kountry, handsome as ever. His spirit must have felt mine. I had not stepped a foot in the door when his very strong "You are so sexy" smile was illuminating his face. We locked eyes; my body was instantly infused with butterflies. My happiness was undeniable. I could not have hidden it even if I'd tried. He made me weak. It felt like my feet had lifted from the ground, and our bodies just met. I didn't even realize I'd made it into his arms. The aroma of his cologne hit my nose.

"How are you, *hermosa*?" he asked so calmly.

"Great!" I said as he released his grip.

He walked over to the counter with me, and we made small talk as I ordered.

"Are you busy today? Are you in a rush? You know we should take this opportunity the universe gives us to catch up!"

I took a minute to think. *Is it worth it? Should I?*

"So?" His eyes sparkled, and he had the most innocent look on his face.

"Fiiine!" I replied.

"Ana!" the barista yelled.

I made my way to grab my tea. Kountry's hand locked in mine, and he was pulling me out the door.

We drove to a nearby park and talked for hours. We could always do that. We talked about everything. We sat there and stared up at the stars and wondered aloud about what it would have been like if we had met in a different life. We both chuckled at the mere thought and then fell into silence.

"You know, I've been meaning to talk to you." He broke the silence.

"Oh yeah? What about?"

"You know my brother Travis?" he asked.

"Mm-hmm." I nodded in response.

"He met this guy that goes by the name of Corona. He's cool—we do business. I think you can get some really good deals. You know, just a thought. Throwing it out there. We can be like business partners," he said as he tried to make eye contact.

"I see." I looked away and avoided his gaze.

It was late, and I had some things to do the next morning, so I soon cut our talk short and told him I would think about his proposition and let him know.

CHAPTER 13:
At the Top

Mornings were my favorite time of the day. Waking up at five o'clock to meditate, stretch, and work out—my every-day routine.

One morning, a couple of weeks after Kountry made his proposition, I finally decided that I would give his idea a chance. Something within me said it was not a good idea, but something else was drawing me to the idea. I gave him a call and told him to set something up with his connection, and we would discuss business.

I received a call early Saturday morning. We planned to meet up at Corona's lake house and take his boat for a spin. I didn't mind the idea of a day spent in a bathing suit out in the beaming heat. I loved the idea.

As I arrived at the address provided, I noticed a very beautiful white house. The gate was a good distance from the home, and as we got closer to the house, I was mesmerized by its beauty, the nature around it, the lake out back, and the number of flowers that lined the pathway. It was like something out of a fairy tale.

Kountry met me outside and walked over to my car to open the door. I felt his energy—he was happy. He opened my door, leaned in, and said, "Good morning, hermosa." With a peck on the cheek, he greeted me.

I followed him as he led me into an open-concept living room decorated with bright colors. The room was illuminated from the gigantic window near the back of the home.

"Hola. Vato!" another man—whom I assumed was Corona— yelled from the top of the stairs.

They greeted each other as if they'd known one another their whole lives. I just chuckled at the look of happiness Kountry had.

"Oh, wow, she is gorgeous!" Corona said as his eyes outlined the curves of my body and ended at my cold stare. He was a tall, tan man, with muscle but with a slight belly due to the amount of beer he drank. Hence the name. He had a long dark mustache and wore expensive name-brand clothes—a silk yellow patterned T-shirt that matched well with the dark-brown slacks and some very expensive crocodile dress shoes with pointed squares at the tip.

"Hola, Corona. *Mucho gusto.*" I leaned in for a greeting kiss on the cheek.

"I told you, bro!" Kountry laughed.

"Shall we?" Corona led the way outside and into his boat.

We discussed business deals, and Corona agreed to bless me with some good prices only because I was a close friend of

Kountry's. I wasn't sure what he owed or what Kountry had over him, but I sensed it was something big. Kountry always held leverage on people.

"Ana, have you ever thought about expanding your business?" Corona had a way of saying things with aggression and passion. He was a top dog and was used to attention. No wonder he got along with Kountry.

I responded to him with a simple nod.

The day was filled with the sun's constant sting on my skin, and I'd forgotten to pack my sunscreen. "For sure I have a sunburn," I kept saying to myself. I felt it all over my body.

The moonlight brought a cool breeze. The wind slivered around my body. Kountry and I sat on the deck of the boat drinking wine, still in our bathing suits. We sat on the ground over a bright tie-dyed blanket. We talked for hours.

We lay back and looked up at the stars.

"What happened to Corona?" I asked, noticing that I hadn't heard his loud voice in a while.

"Not sure. Passed out somewhere around here." He chuckled. "I love you, hermosa," he whispered.

He leaned over and started to caress my thigh. I just lay there and allowed him to seduce my body into the temptation of guilty pleasure.

He slowly made his way over to me. Trying not to put all his weight on me, he laid his heavy body over mine.

"I've been waiting so long to do this," he said as he made his way to kiss me. His weight over my body felt good, like a blanket over me. His kiss was sensual and passionate. We made love for many hours. I fell asleep in his arms under the stars, under the moon, under the universe itself.

"Here's some coffee just like you like it," I heard someone say. I could feel the sun in my face, and my head was already beginning to pulsate. Immediately the guilt began to take over me. I sat there in silence as I drank my coffee, and all I could say and think to myself was *Really? Not again. I need to get out of here.* The minute Kountry got up, I hurriedly grabbed my stuff and put my clothes on.

"Hey, good morning. How did you sleep?" Corona asked, staring at me with a perverted grin on his face, as if he had been watching me the whole time.

"Hey, good morning." I faked a smile.

Once we got back to Corona's house, he invited us to come in for breakfast, but I chose not to. Kountry walked outside to see me off.

That was the beginning of our trio.

Our first deal went smoothly. I sent some of my guys to meet some of Corona's guys. Corona threw in a little surprise—coke. Up to then, I had only negotiated with marijuana. I had been asked about coke before—whether I could cop some, if I knew someone, if I myself would negotiate for it. I felt like that was just not my thing. Corona was smart—he knew what he was doing. He knew I would have to get rid of it. He piqued my interest. I did just that; I had my guys contact some people, and within hours, it was gone. Not only had we just doubled our income, but the demand was greater, and the sale was faster.

You see, I knew this was not a good idea. I had been able to maintain a low profile and was focused on my other business. Yet the temptation was great.

The money was flowing in, and after a year of working with the same partners, I felt that I could trust them. I would step away and focus on my legitimate event-planning business. Kongo stepped up and got the job done. No one messed with him. He was grateful to me for opening this door for him—it was the most money he'd ever made.

I told Kountry about Kongo. He felt that Kongo could not be trusted, but he wouldn't tell me why he felt that way, so I disregarded it as jealousy. Kountry and I started to get close again, and he would act as my personal bodyguard. I once again began to trust him, and he started to get involved in my business. Eventually he and Kongo were running the show.

It was now November 2018, and I had been booked for event planning every weekend since the summer. I was contacted by an agent who had a client coming into town to perform—a singer. He wanted me to set up an event. Not for the singer but for the singer's niece, who was celebrating her birthday. I came highly recommended, and they wanted to book me for that weekend. I was asked to prep an Airbnb for her arrival and birthday celebration. I normally did not do last-minute events, but due to the high profile of the client, I didn't think twice. This would be my big breakthrough. I could expand my business.

I worked nonstop that whole week, hardly getting any sleep. The day of the event came, and the niece loved it! She loved everything about her celebration. The agent called me early that Sunday morning. He thanked me and asked if I could drop off the key at a condo later that day. That Sunday was spent with my kids—a wonderful end to my great weekend. My youngest son lived near the location where I was supposed to drop off the key, so I dropped him off last. On the ride home, he told me how much he missed me and how he couldn't wait to be together again. I dropped him off, and that sentiment resonated in my head. I realized I was not taking care of what had once brought me life and happiness—the ones who had saved my life.

I drove to the location. It was late, so I was in a hurry. I knocked on the door, and a woman opened the door to greet me. She thanked me and took the key. As I drove off, it felt like I had run over something. I quickly pulled over to the side of the road. I got out of my car and bent down to see what was under there.

There was a sudden blow to my head.

CHAPTER 14: Awakening

The throbbing of my head was unbearable. I just sat in silence, pretending to be passed out. I could hear someone say, "We got her. On the way."

I tried to keep a map in my head of the turns we took. We finally made a stop.

"Wake up, bitch." That was followed by a slap to my face.

My hands were tied behind my back, and my legs were bound together. I had a blindfold on to keep me from seeing my captors. I could not move much. The realization that something bad was about to happen hit. I was confused and did not know what was going on. A big man grabbed me and carried me into a motel room. Even though I could not see, I could smell the cheap fragrance permeating the room. He tossed me on the bed and walked out. I could not make out what they were saying—it was muffled, but I could hear the tension in their voices. I was trying to stay calm, but my thoughts kept taking me to a dark place.

The time passed, and I could no longer hear the men. I was confused as to what I was doing there and who we were waiting on. I dozed off. I woke to a bucket of cold water being spilled on my face. I shot up in shock while trying to catch my breath. And that was when it started. The men did not say anything—I just felt the first blow to the face and then one after another. I could barely move due to being tied up. The steady blows distracted my captor from what I was doing, so I managed to loosen the zip tie around my wrists, and it eventually tore. He didn't realize that my hands were loose. The blindfold had fallen off my face, and I could see the room. The moment that the zip tie fell off, I lunged over the side of the bed and grabbed the lamp. I broke it over his head, and with all the power inside of me, I fought back. With no control, I went animalistic. He ran out of the room with blood gushing from his head. Another blow was delivered to my head by another of the captors, and once again I was out. I woke up in the tub as bleach was being poured all over me. It first felt warm, but it soon began to burn. They waterboarded me for hours and still would not tell me what they wanted. The feeling of dying and being brought back to life was unbearable. I started telling them to just kill me. I knew they wanted something. "Y'all better kill me now, because if I ever get out of here alive, I will . . ."

The man I'd hit with the lamp came back, anger in his eyes. He held a towel over the wound as he calmly stated, "I need you to make a phone call and have someone bring one hundred thousand dollars in cash."

"Fuck you." I spit in his face.

Another blow.

What they did not know was that I had mastered the art of controlling my physical pain due to the abuse I'd endured as a kid. They would have to kill me before I would let them get what they wanted.

He threw me back in the bedroom after another beating. I was incoherent but could still make out what they were saying.

"It wasn't supposed to take this long. She is going to die soon. What are we going to do?"

I lay on that cold floor, my eyes nearly bruised shut. I noticed a light from in between the mattress and the wall. It was my phone. It must have fallen out of my pocket at one point. I slowly crawled over to it and began calculating my next steps. As soon as I picked up the phone, they would notice the light. I knew that my phone had the lock screen set up to make an emergency call if needed, but I would still need to dial. I knew it wouldn't work. I couldn't dial fast enough. I had no other choice, though—I had to try. I lunged for the phone, and before I could dial, it flew out of my hand.

"I'm tired of you, bitch. Before I kill you, I'mma have fun with you," one of the men taunted as he kicked my stomach repeatedly. I could hear the zipper of his pants, and I knew what was about to happen. I unattached myself from that situation. I lay on my stomach as I felt the force penetrate inside of me. The tears ran down my face, and as I lay there, I thought about my life. I thought about my choices. I thought about my kids and those last words my son had said.

He finished. Turned me around and began to choke me. I didn't put up a fight. I knew my time was up. Once you accept death, it is peaceful. I saw all my memories flash before my eyes. My life was slowly rewinding in my head, frame by frame like a videotape. The last image was my mother's face looking down at me, a smile on her face and a consoling, comforting look in her eyes—the day I was born. I felt the small smirk on my face as I let go.

I'd always said I knew I had a purpose in life.

A loud bang like a firecracker echoed. I could see lights, but I couldn't make anything out.

"Ma'am, can you hear me? Ma'am, we are here to help. Stay with us."

God held on to me.

A couple of days later, an officer told me they'd received a 911 call from the motel room. When they'd first arrived, they'd knocked, and after no response, they'd been about to leave, but one of the cops had had an uneasy feeling and had broken in.

That was all I needed to disappear. I left everything behind and moved away. I told no one except for my kids and my sister.

Not long after this happened, I sat at the edge of a bridge with the idea of jumping.

"Why are you still holding on to me?" I asked God.

Memories of my lifetime began to appear, and I started to make sense of some things as I changed my mind and came down from the bridge. On the way home I sat at a red light, and when it suddenly turned green, I pressed on the gas and ran into the car in front of me. I looked up again, and the light was back on red. I was confused—I could have sworn it had turned green. Nevertheless, I pulled over to a gas station to make sure everything was okay. An old lady got out of the other car. I didn't know why, but I began to cry and apologize to her, letting her know I'd had a bad day. She allowed me to talk, and when I'd finished, she asked if she could pray over me. It was amazing. I instantly felt better. Before we parted ways, she told me not to worry about the car.

On the way home, I took the same route as always. This time was different; the street I normally took had been blocked, and I was redirected to another street. I got the sudden feeling that something was off. The grass alongside the road actively grew longer and longer before my eyes. I was so confused—I had never seen grass grow like this before.

Where am I? I wondered. I drove on this strange street for a good mile. It soon ended, and I was back on a familiar street. The next day as I was driving home, everything looked normal. In an attempt to find that street, I took the same detour as before, but to my surprise the road with the long grass was not there. There was not one sign of such a street existing. I was so confused.

It has been years since this experience. I write today in hopes that someone could tell me what was going on. I have opened my eyes to realize I am a spiritual being experiencing a human life.

I know I chose my path for a reason. I inhabited this world with a mission. I have been blinded for so long by the temptations of this world, which have held me back. I need answers. I need to figure out what my mission is. Where did I come from? Why am I here?

www.ingramcontent.com/pod-product-compliance
Lightning Source LLC
Chambersburg PA
CBHW062027040426
42447CB00010B/2172